D1264072

THE KING PENGUIN BOOKS

55

ROMNEY MARSH

Romney Marsh

ILLUSTRATED

AND DESCRIBED

BY

JOHN PIPER

PENGUIN BOOKS

1950

THE KING PENGUIN BOOKS

EDITOR: N. B. L. PEVSNER · TECHNICAL EDITOR: R. B. FISHENDEN

PUBLISHED BY

PENGUIN BOOKS LIMITED, HARMONDSWORTH, MIDDLESEX, ENGLAND

AND BY PENGUIN BOOKS PTY LTD, 200 NORMANBY ROAD

MELBOURNE, AUSTRALIA

FIRST PUBLISHED 1950

To Karen and Osbert Lancaster

TEXT PAGES PRINTED BY R. AND R. CLARK LTD, EDINBURGH

PLATES MADE AND PRINTED BY JOHN SWAIN AND SON LTD, BARNET

MADE IN GREAT BRITAIN

SOME EARLIER VIEWS

—

'Are any of you artists as well as archaeologists? If only the weather favour us, you will scarcely need Mr Champneys's charming book to introduce you to the picturesque effects of pasture land and dyke scenery. Our Kentish Holland lacks, I fear, its Cuyp or Wouvermans, but Mr Champneys in his able word-and-pencil sketches has done something to show us what a painter might achieve out of very simple materials. Even such an one as I, who have no artistic tinglings in my finger tips, have more than once felt myself stirred to admire the poetry of a Marsh landscape. True, it has fallen to my lot to view it through a thick veil of mist, and in drenching rain, as well as in one of the heaviest gales of the last ten years. At such times the picturesque side of the prospect comes scarcely uppermost.

'But take our Roman-ey, this Roman Marsh of ours, in one of its calmer, brighter, happier moods. The sun, let me say, is hasting to his setting over Fairlight, and the shadows are lengthening out Hythe-wards. A gentle evening breeze rustles peacefully among the flags along the dyke-side. The blue sky overhead was never more blue. Where are we? Is this Kent? Are we in England at all? Or have we dropped down somewhere on the Campagna, outside the walls of Rome? For lack of a ruined aqueduct your eye falls on the grey wall of Hope, or Eastbridge, or on the solitary arch of Midley. On the one side rises a tall landmark across the plain, the Campanile of Lydd; on the other stretches far away the long ridge of the Alban and Sabine hills, which folk hereabout call Lympne and Aldington. But I know better, for, while my friend the Marsh Rector and I are still arguing the point, there comes creaking along the road to Ostia (New Romney, he calls it) a heavy waggon drawn by the wide-horned, mild-eyed, melancholy oxen, which every Roman artist knows so well.'

Dr Parry, Bishop of Dover, in an Address to the
Kent Archaeological Society, July 1879.

'The scenery of Romney Marsh is not at once so striking as one might expect, but it is really of singular beauty, and possesses a charm which certainly increases on renewed acquaintance. Seen from a passing ship, the marshland looks flat and uninteresting, and no one would be very enthusiastic in its praise. The solitary lighthouse at Dungeness, standing on what looks like a narrow bank of shingle, presents a curiously desolate picture. The waves are crushed into white, boiling foam on the pebbly shore, the wind whistles in weird melancholy cadence across the expanse of marsh and water.

The whole scene produces on the mind a rather uncomfortable impression of barrenness and desolation.

'To see the beauties of the Marsh one must walk or drive about its quaint old-fashioned villages, or ascend the lofty towers of New Romney Church or Lydd Church; or, still better, view the land from the commanding heights near Lympne, where a glorious, comprehensive panorama of the whole of Romney Marsh and the adjacent country is spread out at the beholder's feet.'

George Clinch, in *Memorials of Old Kent*, 1907.

'As you drive along a road bounded by deep cuttings fringed with a deep-brown funereal reed, it is borne in upon you that the scene is as beautiful as it is strange. As you look over field upon field into distance upon distance, recognised solely by delicate atmospheric change, and see each willow a little greyer, and the tile-roof of each homestead a little less red, and each haystack a shade less golden than the nearer one, till all fades into a shadowy fringe in which individual objects are matters for conjecture, a sense of space and of mystery steals over you which might have inspired David Cox or De Wint; then further, as you watch remote objects and unconsciously guess at their relative distances, and a sense of motion in one or more of them gains upon you, and finally you become aware that they are ships in full sail in the offing and on the same level as the trees and the haystacks and only a little more distant: then the sense of strangeness and the sense of amphibiousness rush together, and you feel as detached from the ordinary interests of the world and as amphibious as the oldest inhabitant.

'It is just this kind of sentiment in landscape, this sense of personal identification with the physical conditions of the soil, which is the most penetrating, the most wholesome, and therefore the most permanent charm; it is this which has been and will be the motive of the truest art of external nature; and it proceeds neither from grandeur of scale nor ruggedness of outline nor from a vivid clearness of atmosphere nor from any special or exotic conditions whatever, but grows up in the simplicity and grave harmony of native scenes, and demands no energy and no effort, but only a little sensitiveness and a little sympathy.'

Basil Champneys, *A Quiet Corner of England*, 1875.

'I have stayed on Romney Marsh and have watched the eastern sky darken across the dyked flats to Dymchurch and the Channel towards the French coast as the sun set at my back, and have noticed the strange unity of sea, sky and earth that grows unnoticed at this time and place.'

Paul Nash, Autobiographical article, *c*. 1940.

ROMNEY MARSH

—

In its flatness and sense of remoteness quite unlike the rest of the beautiful county to which it belongs, Romney Marsh yet bears plenty of Kentish traces. The weather-boarded houses, the trim fences and trimmer hedges, the poplars and the long-roofed, odd-shaped Kentish churches are there. And it has the absence of barrenness, the look of having been used and almost over-used by man, that belongs to the rest of the county.

In the Marsh, you are seldom out of sight of a church, though most of the churches are in fact partly hidden in their tree-screens. The two best total views of this remarkable landscape are those from the old cliff-edge near Lympne, above Stutfall Castle, and from the grassy knoll in Oxney to the south of Stone church. From either of these points you can take in at one look most of the Marsh and, on a clear day, the coast of France with Dungeness dimming away towards it. Grassland still predominates greatly in the view (in spite of the recent increase in arable); flocks of the famous Romney Marsh sheep dot wide patches of landscape. The villages with their churches are in knots of elm, alder and willow, and some of the connecting roads are lined with the remainder – and the total is not very large – of the well-grown trees. There is not much in these comprehensive views to indicate the history of the landscape and former waterscape, for the rises in the ground that speak of former dryness in the waste of water are rises of only a few feet, and not detectable from a distance.

There is an absence – considering that this is a drained marsh – of straight lines. The foreground tree-fringed Royal Military Canal and the distant coastlines are noticeable for their straightness. But the Rother river curves, many of the dykes curve, the boundary hedges and fences are not straight for long. Water lies in light-coloured snatches and loops that reflect a winter sky much more often than in straight furrows. This is because the dykes and dammings were done piecemeal, holdings were shaped in relation to them and tracks planned in relation to holdings and settlements. There are stretches of straight road, but they are short, and often terminate at right-angle bends.

Other things that might be noticed are the shapes of the blown trees, the rich warmth of colour at any season, and the signs of wartime defence work in this nearest-the-continent country; the dark blots of the Martello Towers along the east marsh coast from Hythe away past Littlestone, the Military Canal, and the remains of twentieth-century war activity – rusty wire in hedgerows, Radar masts and an occasional crow's-nest look-out on the coast. With a little imagination and a map one can trace – from Stone – the line of the road from Appledore to New Romney, a road that roughly follows the line of the Rhee Wall which created the original, proper Romney Marsh. The author of *Murray's Handbook*, looking from the heights in the middle of last century, found that 'the line of the ancient estuary, which, beyond Dymchurch, passed inland as far as Lympne, is readily traceable by the eye, as the sand with which the soil is filled contrasts strongly in colour with the rich pastures southward'. But 'readily traceable' would be too strong a phrase today.

There is extraordinary richness of summer vegetation, the grass is lush and the dykes and banks, when uncut, are thick with reeds and waterplants. In winter the reeds still blow in the dykes, showing a pale-yellow flank of close stalks with feathery crowns of grey or purple-black fronds, and there are pea-stacks, built on a tripod of sticks for aeration, as well as the many dyke-side potato and swede clamps. The fences are mostly made of three long split oak or elm rails joining stout posts, the whole low and sturdy, and they grow an emerald lichen that at first seems to dust, and finally screens the pale-grey wood. They are an important feature in marsh colour, and very often the palest objects in the view. They look excellent against the blackthorn hedges in winter when these are dark purple-brown, and against the oranges and reds of massed willow branches. The levels themselves are often paler than the sky – a fact that has been too heavily underlined by some modern film directors who have photographed scenes under Romney Marsh skies with red-filter cloud effects. The most frequent and the most characteristic views in the Marsh have foregrounds of pale warmth, distances of misted trees and low hills, and intervening low levels in pale light.

The draught oxen, so common here till the present century, have gone, the water-draining windmills are gone (the last not long ago) and dusty or muddy un-tarred roads have mostly gone, too. Nowadays tractors backfire in the fields, telegraph poles are more common than trees, radio masts than church towers – and much taller – and the Marsh has only its character and colour and light to distinguish it from any other English marsh. But it is distinguished enough.

The Marsh has been famous for a very long time for rich pastures – some of them the richest in England. What is special about them is the predominance in them of perennial rye-grass and white clover, and the absence of 'weeds' (miscellaneous species). 'The total flora usually comprises less than twenty-five species of flowering plants (of which the majority are grasses), and sometimes no more than twenty ... In Leicestershire pastures rye-grass and white clover constitute from half to nearly three-quarters of the herbage, in the Blackmoor Vale from a quarter to a half, and in Romney Marsh from a third to nine-tenths.' (Tansley.)

The local breed of sheep, the 'Kent' or 'Romney Marsh', has been bred for many generations to suit the special local conditions, the rich herbage and the exposed, wind-blown character of the grazing grounds. More sheep to the acre can be fattened in the best of the Marsh meadows than anywhere else in England. Parts of the Marsh in summer seem to be (in Shenstone's words) 'white over with sheep'; in winter there are not so many, for some of them, including the yearling lambs, are moved inland. The wealthy stock farmers used to be called the 'Romney Kings', and, though it is not so easy to make a fortune now as a sheep farmer on the Marsh, the Romney Marsh breed still has a great name outside as well as inside the country, especially in New Zealand and Australia. Isolated shepherds' huts – always of much the same pattern, of one room with a gabled tiled roof and with a chimney at one end – are prominent everywhere. Cobbett was excited when he saw the sheep on his Rural Ride across the Marsh from Appledore to Hythe in September 1823. He calls them 'very pretty and large. The wethers, when fat, weigh about twelve stone, or one hundred pounds. The faces of these sheep are white; and indeed the whole sheep is as white as a piece of writing paper. The wool does not look dirty and oily like that of other sheep.'

At present the sheep farming here is on the decline. This, the best of grazing land, is also among the best arable, and much of it was ploughed up during the Hitler war, and more has been ploughed since. There is very little loss of beauty, if any; for burgeoning root crops and waving cornlands on these lowlands have as much beauty, and look as personal to the neighbourhood, as the lush grasslands.

Romney Marsh is a generic name, but was never the only name, and is still not the only map-name, of the levels between Hythe and Rye that are bounded on the landward side by the low hills behind the Military Canal. The area includes Romney Marsh proper (nearly 24,000 acres), Walland Marsh, Denge Marsh and Guldeford Level (together, about 22,600 acres) – the last, with East Guldeford village and the vanished village of Broomhill, in Sussex.

There is so much doubt about the origin and development of the whole area, and so many important points have not been settled (and many points now are questioned that had long been thought to be settled), that the statement of a few isolated facts about which there are not many remaining doubts is necessary.

Probably there was never a time when the whole area was covered by the sea at low tide; that is, not a recent geological time. In early historical times there was a great bay of the Channel at Romney and a smaller bay by West Hythe and Lympne, extending as a narrow arm of sea to Appledore and Rye by the line of the present Military Canal; while wooded peninsulas between Appledore and Fairlight and islands at Oxney, Rye and Winchelsea divided other arms of the sea that flowed inland at high tide, the sea never receding far enough at low tide to leave the flooded areas 'in any state but that of a soft loose residuum through which the rivers wound their way'. (Holloway.) So that the old cliffs to the west and north of the present-day Marsh were only in places true sea cliffs, and the area was riddled with enormous tidal creeks and unhealthy marshes. The Romans used Portus Lemanis, which was probably under Lympne, by Stutfall Castle, as a port (it is mentioned in the Antonine Itinerary). The picturesque ruins of the castle – low broken walls – lie scattered up the cliffside towards Lympne, across the Royal Military Canal. Most authorities credit the Romans with the first bold reclamation scheme. This scheme was the building of the Rhee Wall from Appledore to Romney, and the Dymchurch Wall along the east coast, which first enclosed and defined what is still Romney Marsh proper. It seems fairly certain that there was already a measure of shingle protection (possibly of the present Chesil Beach kind) where the Dymchurch Wall now stands; and that the marshes grew up inside the protecting shingle – with much assistance from man. Outside the area, by the eighth century Romney was an island at high water, with a wide strip of land extending towards Hope.

Much discussion has gone on, and still goes on, about the probable early courses of the Limen, or Rother river. It may have changed its course twice and it has certainly changed it once. Before the eleventh century it may have flowed out at Hythe – or rather, West Hythe – the Saxon-named renewal of the Roman Portus Lemanis. Certainly from the eleventh to the sixteenth centuries it flowed out at Romney, adopting roughly the present line of the Rhee Wall from Appledore. After that it changed again, and took the shorter route to the sea which it still follows, flowing out at Rye Harbour. This change was partly owing to the silting up of the bed, but also because of a storm, or storms. Lambarde, the Kent historian, and others after him add an 'earthquake' to the causes.

Romney was one of the Cinque Ports, the others being Hastings, Sandwich, Hythe and Dover; Rye and Winchelsea were added later. In the thirteenth century the Cinque Ports undertook the naval defence of the country and were granted special privileges in return. They were much concerned in the wars against the French, and dealt with piratical raids.

The Marsh and its coast have seen more smuggling than any other area in the country. There were various forms. Wool-running to France was the chief. Fuller's earth was also exported illegally at one time. Brandy, silks and lace were the usual illegal imports. Legislation against importing wool began in the fourteenth century, and absolute prohibition was decided on in the reign of Charles II. Romney Marsh smuggling then increased enormously. By the middle of the eighteenth century most of the population of the Marsh was either directly concerned in, or else connived at smuggling; and there was a general laxity about money and morals. Handselling was in vogue, and the marriage of maidens almost unknown. There is a well-known local story, often laughed at by guide-book writers, about the wooden detached belfry of Brookland church leaping off the church into the churchyard in surprise at a young couple presenting themselves at the church to be married – a story that is at least two centuries old. And there are very few churches in the Marsh that are not traditionally spoken of as storehouses for smuggled goods. Empty but lidded stone coffins at Ivychurch and elsewhere are pointed out as former hiding-places for liquor, as well as for the corpses of men who had been murdered. The land smugglers collected wool from inland for transport across the Channel from the Marsh coast, and they went in companies thirty or so strong. The most formidable was the 'Hawkhurst Gang' which operated before 1747, when a band of local Militia was formed and fought them out of existence, some of the gang retiring to Dorset.

The Martello towers along the coast were put up by order of Pitt's Parliament in 1804 as part of the defence scheme against Napoleonic invasion, the Royal Military Canal (which might have served as a tank trench in the war) being another part of it. The form and name of the towers were suggested by a fort of a similar kind that the British had stormed with difficulty at Mortella in Corsica. They cost between £10,000 and £20,000 each to build.

Work on the Royal Military Canal was begun in 1807, the bank formed from the excavations being thrown up on the side away from the sea, in order to screen readily lines of defending infantry. For almost the whole course, the canal is planted with elm trees (here and there are some ash), sometimes in a single and sometimes a double line; and it is these trees in their straight stretches that add such character to this inland side of the Marsh, in both close and distant views. For a great distance they shade unmetalled roads that run parallel with them. The canal was adapted to carry troops and stores, and for some years in the nineteenth century a packet-boat ran on it. In the early nineties (according to the fifth edition of *Murray's Handbook*) it was still being used for the transport of road material. 'An Act was passed in 1867 allowing the Secretary at War to dispose of it, and a project has been mooted to convert a part of its bed into a railway, connecting Hythe with London by a line through the Weald. Small houses, erected at intervals of about two miles, are mostly occupied by pensioners of the Ordnance Department who act as "walksmen", and exercise a kind of supervision of the Traffic.' (Murray, *ibid.*)

The sea, nowhere visible from the levels, is very close in fact and influence. On the eastern coastline bungalows, villas and the huts of holiday camps are as near together as beads on a necklace all the way from Hythe to Dungeness. The cliff-less coastline has a fringe of shingle on the seaward side of the Marsh embankment, and at low tide a stretch of fine sand. As far as Littlestone the bungalows hide down behind the sea wall, the Martello towers only eyeing the sea from above it.

Dymchurch, the first connected settlement down the coast from Hythe, has lost one character and found another. It has lost the charm it had when H. G. Wells described it in *Kipps* – the charm of a small classless village by the sea with a wide deserted beach and a waste of marsh on three sides. It has found the new character of seaside suburbanism, which is too easily despised, and which is the commonest seaside character in England today. The radio shop, the Tudor teahouse with stained beams, 1930 inglenook, and uncut lawn at the back; the antique shops, the restored pubs, the double-decker bus service, the headlights on the tarmac and the constant sound of a distant wireless, all are there. So are the relics of the past – just enough to distinguish it from a coast village in Lincolnshire or West Sussex – the restored, tiled Kent church, the weather-boarding and tile-hanging of the older cottages, showing between the pollarded trees. And on each side stretch suburbs, strung out thinly under the sea wall or on the level of the beach, looking jaunty but afraid of the breakers, temporarily shattered by war, waiting for the rare peace and sun and summer.

Littlestone-on-Sea looks braver, and in fact it was a bit too brave. It was first laid out in 1886 and developed in the nineties, and has a short and sweet front of tall imposing lodging-houses with respectable steps and verandahs and dormers, and it is like a short section – a quarter of a mile or so – of Scarborough or Paignton, cut off sharply at both ends. At its back, towards the station and New Romney, is an area of adopted and unadopted roads that serve holiday houses that have become all-the-year-round houses. The effect is like that of any small seaside place of an Edwardian, or just pre-Edwardian, date, but the appearance (owing to a number of sudden end-walls, and unfinished-looking schemes) is tinged by a sense of former sad scenes in solicitors' offices and perhaps in Carey Street. There is a total effect of Littlestone not having lived up to some hopes. It has a decayed charm, as well as a lively present-day life; and a celebrated golf course.

Beyond Littlestone, until after the 1914-18 war, there was no development along the coast, but then came new suburban houses placed on and above the shingle in an untidy frayed ribbon. This has developed into Greatstone, St Mary's Bay and Lydd-on-Sea (the last two named from the old villages inland). Seen across a stretch of marsh the houses take their place. At close range they are like a treeless and shrubless collection of the houses that line any by-pass out of London. They all date from the nineteen-thirties, and as a small exhibition of the popular architecture of the period they could not be bettered. Instead of backing on to a suburban electric railway they back on to the Romney, Hythe and Dymchurch miniature railway, which has its terminus at Greatstone, and beyond that there fades away the waste of shingle inland to Lydd. A few of their names indicate their character: *Hove To*, *Windy Cot*, *Midships*, *Galleons*, *Owl's Retreat*, *Per Mart* (*Percy*, *Martha*, perhaps), *Mount Nod*, *Cooparoo*, *Linga Longa*, *Sea Spray*, *Sea Close*, *Sea Wynd*, *Minarest*, *Thistledome* (*This'tle do me*), *Twix Us*, *Emohruo* (*Our Home*, backwards), *Ecnamor* (*Romance* backwards), *Nelande* (*Edna*, *Len* backwards).

Towards Dungeness itself the character changes. Fishermen and coastguards live here, and the holiday-makers of the older-fashioned kind. The dwellings are almost all wooden huts or disused railway carriages, set down slap on the shingle, some little way back from the sea, not indecently near it, as at Greatstone. Many of them have been decorated ingeniously, in an attempt to make them as gay as a barge or a roundabout at a fair. The lighthouse, black-and-white striped, with its white outbuildings with black chimneys – as gay in its Trinity House manner as the shacks – dominates everything. The thin concrete road disappears inland to Lydd with a close rank of telegraph poles beside it: once off this road and you crunch across shingle, aided here and there for a step by tiny islands of marram-grass.

The romance of this small, blank, isolated neck of land is strong. The shingle point has been extending into the sea for years – probably for hundreds of years; but nobody knows for how long, or precisely how the shingle that builds it up travels across the wide bay from the west – from Fairlight, towards Hastings – as some of it does. The rate of extension is apparently lessening. The sharpness of the point is explained by the sudden change in exposure to two prevailing winds. The big waves come up the Channel from the Atlantic, or from the North Sea, and the two shores face them. The nearness of the coast of France does not allow waves of any size to develop when the wind blows directly *at* the point, from a south-easterly direction; and in any case there is not a prevailing wind from that direction.

Large ships come quite close inshore rounding Dungeness and it is always said that more ships can be seen passing the point than can be seen in the same time from any other place in the world. There are also a good many wrecks, some of the more spectacular Victorian ones being illustrated by early photographs in cork and walnut frames in the two or three inns along the coast. During the recent war one of the pipelines for the supply of petrol abroad crossed the Channel from a point close to the Ness, and storage tanks were disposed in many of the living-rooms and garages of the Lydd-on-Sea houses, their fronts or sides being removed to receive them.

There was a beacon in early times near the place where the lighthouse now stands: first a stack of wood, then a standard with a pitch-pot. Until the nineteenth century the lighthouse belonged to the Earls of Leicester, one of whom erected it.

Because of the absence of sand, the southerly beach from Dungeness to Camber is almost deserted. The shingle shelves steeply into twenty or thirty fathoms of water (thirty-three fathoms close to the shore at the Ness itself), and big waves pitch on to it in a gale. The place that is most like it is the Chesil Beach in Dorset, from Portland Island to Abbotsbury, but the shingle there is larger, and even more difficult to walk on. The lights and colour across this beach are as unexpected and as much themselves as those on the Marsh. Inland towards Lydd the shingle is a pale, warm brown, and is patched with the bright green of brooms and gorse and the pale washed-out yellow of marram-grass, and, in summer, is rashed here and there with foxgloves. The beach between high- and low-water marks is oyster-grey with white and yellow lights, and has a wriggling line of seaweed and driftwood near its crest. The buildings and jetties of Rye Harbour, with Rye itself on its low hill, are seen to the west, and far away is Fairlight Hill on the skyline. To the east, beyond the lighthouse, is the open Channel.

Inland there are short and inconsequent stretches of concrete road made by the War Department to reach gunnery-practice ranges, and there are older roads across the shingle leading to collections of huts and coastguard houses – Hope and Anchor and Galloways.

The shingle between Lydd and the south coast is waved in faintly-raised, wide curves which lie in bow shapes. Here and there, in the tank-training region known as Holmstone, are holly trees growing close to the ground, large, but having fought for centuries against gusty winds. Their presence is as surprising to us today as it was to Leland, the sixteenth-century topographer, who remarked them. Otherwise, there are no excrescences on this flat landscape of stones except a water tower, the telegraph poles, the raw houses along the eastern beach at Greatstone and the distant lighthouse with its outbuildings, two or three odd farms (including a large and distinguished one called Brickwall) across the shingle and a few tarred shacks. 'Stunted elder bushes in many parts furnish an excellent cover for hares, which abound and afford good coursing.' (Murray.) There is still a Coursing Club at New Romney, which sends out a club card with a good nineteenth-century engraving often to be seen displayed on mantelpieces and pinned to public bars in the Marsh inns.

Lydd, with its atmosphere of war training, its enormous gaunt village green where villas look over football, and its tall tower in trees, is the only village near Dungeness; and Lydd is nearly four miles away.

New Romney is a town planned in squares and shows visible traces of its medieval history in fragments of walling and details that have been re-used in some buildings. Apart from Lydd and New Romney there are no large villages in the Marsh, except the lately-developed Dymchurch. The usual village plan shows a church, a parsonage, an inn and perhaps half a dozen cottages disposed near a cross-roads, usually with a planted tree screen. Brookland is open, and rather larger than this. The churches will reward the ecclesiologist. New Romney has a remarkable and fine-coloured Norman tower, the churches at Ivychurch and Newchurch are grandly planned, and several churches, including Ivychurch, St Mary's, Old Romney and Brookland, escaped any violent restoration in Victorian times. Brookland belfry is an object of great curiosity, and Fairfield is a twentieth-century rebuilding of great sensibility. The ruined chapels of Hope, Midley, Eastbridge and West Hythe are picturesque fragments.

The domestic architecture of the Marsh is not remarkable. Nowhere on it is there a house as beautiful as the farm at Oxenbridge, for instance, which looks across it from the Cliff; but the use of tile-hanging and weather-boarding gives a good many of the farms and cottages Kentish character. In Lydd and New Romney there is some good straightforward Georgian work in brick, and Basil Champneys in his book sketched some well-detailed internal features. The most characteristic buildings on the Marsh are the square farms with their barns and outbuildings in screens of elm trees, simply planned and harmonious in colour, looking across the wide levels.

SOME BOOKS AND ARTICLES ON THE DISTRICT

(*Subjects indicated in brackets and itals., where not evident from titles. Note: A.C.='Archaeologia Cantiana': i.e., Proceedings of the Kent Archaeological Society*)

KENT HISTORIANS

Leland, Camden, Lambard, Dugdale, Somner, Hasted, Horsfield, Dearne, Victoria County History (in progress).

GENERAL BOOKS AND ARTICLES

Champneys, Basil. *A Quiet Corner of England.* 1875.
Cox, J. C. *Rambles in Kent.* 1913.
Cox, J. C. *Little Guide to Kent.* 1905.
Furley, R. 'Outline History of Romney Marsh', in *A.C.* 13. 1880.
Furley, R. *The Weald of Kent* (2 v.). 1874.
Holloway, Wm. *The History of Romney Marsh.* 1849.
Jerrold, Walter. *Highways and Byways in Kent.* 1907.
Lewis, Arthur D. *The Kent Coast.* 1911.
Mais, S. P. B. *The Land of The Cinque Ports.* 1949.
Murray's Handbook. About 1895 (latest edition).

SPECIAL ASPECTS

Burrows, M. *The Cinque Ports.*
Clinch, Geo., in *Memorials of Old Kent.* (*Smuggling.*
Erwood, F. C. E. 'Notes on the Churches of Romney Marsh', 1923, in *A.C.* 37. 1925. (*Lydd, Hope, Midley, Eastbridge, New Romney, Dymchurch, Burmarsh, St Mary Marsh, Ivychurch, Brenzett, Brookland, Newchurch, Snargate.*)
Gilbert, C. J. 'The Evolution of Romney Marsh', in *A.C.* 45. 1933.
Holmes, T. Rice. *Ancient Britain and the Invasion of Julius Caesar.* (*Evolution of the Marsh.*)
Homan, W. Mark. 'The Marshes between Hythe and Pett', in *Sussex Archaeological Collections*, 79. 1938.
Jessup, R. F. *The Archaeology of Kent.* (*Stutfall Castle.*)
Lewin, T. *The Invasion of England by Julius Caesar.* 2nd edn. 1862. (*Evolution of the Marsh.*)
Lewis, W. V. 'Formation of Dungeness Foreland', in *Geog. Journal.* 1932.

Lewis and Balchin, in *Geog. Journal.* 1940.
Memoirs. *Geological Survey.* 1864.
Robertson, W. A. S. 'Romney old and new', in *A.C.* 13. 1880.
Robertson, W. A. S. 'Churches in Romney Marsh', in *A.C.* 13. 1880. (*Old Romney, Snargate, Lydd, Ivychurch, New Romney, Brookland.*)
Steers, J. A. *The Coastline of England and Wales.* 1946. (*Geology and History.*)
Teichman-Derville, M. *The Level and Liberty of Romney Marsh.* 1936. (*History.*)
Teichman-Derville, M. 'The Romney and Cinque Ports Records', in *A.C.* 42. 1930.

One of the oval text boards, so characteristic of Romney Marsh church interiors, from Ivychurch

NOTES ON THE CHURCHES OF THE MARSH AND THE CLIFF

Bilsington

Bonnington

ALDINGTON. St Martin. Has a very handsome appearance, with its well-weathered and magnificent Perpendicular tower, neighboured by farm buildings. There is some good carved woodwork, and there are thirteenth- and fourteenth-century details – but the church has been so much restored that it has lost most of its interest and beauty.

APPLEDORE. SS. Peter and Paul. The church is a romantic object when seen through the trees of the Royal Military Canal from the Marsh. Successive alterations in the nineteenth century removed much of its beauty. It was originally a thirteenth-century building. There are restored screens.

BILSINGTON. SS. Peter and Paul. A pretty exterior, with a fine view over the Marsh. The bell hangs under a tiled gable in the churchyard. Inside, a little fourteenth-century glass and a lot of pitch-pine; Commandment

Brenzett

boards, and a magnificent Royal Arms (1774) removed to the west end. There is also a good modern (1944) hatchment to Sir A. F. C. C. Luxmoore. But the church lacks 'atmosphere' internally.

BONNINGTON. St Rumwald. This little nave and chancel church is beautifully placed, by itself, near the Canal. It has a pretty exterior with a seventeenth-century bellcote. There has been a good deal of restoration, and the windows are filled with green 'cathedral' glass. It has little antiquarian interest left, but there are some thin thirteenth- and fourteenth-century features. The planting of the churchyard is not suited to the surroundings.

BRENZETT. St Eanswith. The church here is of a pleasant irregular shape with a broach spire (with internal timber framing). It has some respectable details of the thirteenth and fourteenth centuries, but was violently

Brookland

restored and refitted in 1902. The pitch-pine pews are of an ugly shape, and the windows are largely filled with 'cathedral' glass. The eighteenth-century reredos has been removed to the north chapel, in which also is a seventeenth-century tomb with armoured effigy. There are some Marsh-type text boards and a fine Royal Arms.

BROOKLAND. St Augustine. Like many of the churches on the Marsh, Brookland's present beauty is largely a result of the weathering action of wind and rain on a building that grew slowly and has been added to and patched at various times, without suffering any severe restoration, or the expenditure of much money on conscious beautification in the nineteenth and twentieth centuries. It still keeps its box pews and old floors. The lead font (thirteenth-century) has panels containing the signs of the Zodiac and the months. (December is represented by a butcher killing an ox with a hatchet.) The detached bell-tower has lately been restored and covered with shingles, in place of the old tarred weather-boards which decayed. There is a complicated internal structure of criss-crossing joists and supports, 'saltire-wise'. Some fourteenth-century glass survives.

Dymchurch

Burmarsh. All Saints. Simple Norman and fifteenth-century church, much restored. It has a charming exterior, with white and yellow lichen on grey stone walls, and an individual shape. The interior is commonplace, with pitch-pine and poor Victorian glass in the east window. There are one or two small wall monuments, and one oval text with gold scroll border of the Marsh type. A photograph taken before the restoration of 1878, hanging in the church, shows an interior with box pews, high pulpit and simple eighteenth-century reredos.

Dymchurch. SS. Peter and Paul. An irregular building of furbished-up stone, slate and tile, surrounded by pollarded trees beside the main road. The tall Norman chancel arch is the best feature. There are other Norman and thin later features, but the building has been much renewed. The modernized west gallery has a fine Royal Arms hung upon its front.

Eastbridge. Fragment of a ruin, near a farm.

Hope

EAST GULDEFORD (Sussex). Box pews and nineteenth-century wall-paintings enrich a barn-like, buttressed structure of the sixteenth century. It is highly picturesque, but architecturally undistinguished. Decayed late nineteenth-century paintings cover the walls. (Plate 13.)

FAIRFIELD. St Thomas of Canterbury. By itself on the Marsh, and mellowed with yellow lichen. The illustration in Oyler's *Churches of the Diocese of Canterbury* (1912) shows a tottering ruin by the dyke, mostly of timber. W. D. Caröe rebuilt it from the ground in 1913, with great care and sensibility. Some of the old materials were re-used. The box pews, pulpit and reading desk are painted white, picked out in black. The oval text boards add character. (Plates 8, 9.)

HOPE. A ruin of a chapel of All Saints on a dyke-formed island. The church was in decay by 1573 through lack of repairs, and has been a ruin since about the middle of the seventeenth century.

Ivychurch

IVYCHURCH. St George. Owing to the pitting and scoring of the stonework by weather this church takes on the mood of the day in its appearance, looking dark on a grey day and pale and silvery on a clear one. It is large, clerestoried and regularly planned, the aisles being continuous and flanking the chancel as well as nave. The roofs are of pale-grey lead. The church was built about 1370, and the tower added rather later. There is some excellent flowing tracery, especially in the west window of the north aisle, which has some original glass in its tracery lights. (There is also old glass in the east window of the south aisle: canopy work, patched richly with brighter Victorian 'chapel' glass.) The interior has a cool harmony of colours: greys, yellows and whites. The pews have been removed. The choir stalls, with some old work, remain and are backed by Perpendicular screens of a mellow grey colour. Oval texts of the usual Marsh type, in gold on black, are displayed over each pillar of the arcades, and handsome Royal Arms, dated 1775, are over the south door in an equally handsome grey and white frame. The Commandment

Kenardington

boards are on each side of the altar, and the good solid Communion rails have turned balusters. The gates in the low parclose screens have eighteenth-century Chinese-taste gates, and resemble those at Old Romney. The north aisle is partitioned off, and until fairly recently was used as the village school. The locally-carpentered tower screen is dated 1686. There are wide views across the Marsh from the top of the tower. (Plates 10, 11.)

KENARDINGTON. St Mary. The church is on a rise, and is a prominent object from the Marsh. It is a fragment (the aisle) of an original large church which was struck by lightning in the sixteenth century. In its patched-up state it has a certain charm but is not remarkable.

LYDD. All Saints. 'The Cathedral of the Marsh' was severely damaged by enemy action during the Hitler war. The fine Perpendicular tower is undamaged. The church is now (1947) undergoing temporary repairs: the ultimate restoration will need to be heavy. There are some pre-

Midley

Conquest features. Though large, the church was not particularly distinguished.

LYMPNE. St Stephen's. In a splendid situation overlooking the Marsh from the heights. This church was so heavily restored in 1878-80 as to have been almost rebuilt. The square tower was Norman, and is said to have been built by Archbishop Lanfranc with the help of some of the squared stones from Stutfall Castle. The rest originally Early English.

MIDLEY. A tall ruin in fields on a slight rise that was formerly an island. The church was already decayed in the sixteenth century.

NEWCHURCH. SS Peter and Paul. Well placed on a bank with willows; a good landmark from the north-west. Like a less grand Ivychurch in appearance. The tower leans outwards in an alarming manner. Good tracery in some windows (see cut in *Archaeologia Cantiana*, 13) and good external texture, in spite of repointing. Spacious interior, but one without

Newchurch

positive character: yellow-washed, and with views through clear-glass windows of neighbouring elms and willows. Fittings late Victorian. There are fragments of old glass and of wood-carving. Good Victorian glass is in the east window. Nave and aisles, west tower, north and south porches – the wide north porch is tunnel-like and effective.

NEW ROMNEY. St Nicholas. The fine brown and yellow stone Norman tower dominates the town. The rest of the church is Norman and Decorated. The interior has a good effect, with its white columns and round arches above the dark Victorian box pews. The effect is somewhat spoiled by three poor stained-windows, including the east window, and by the rippled glass above the seventeenth-century tower screen. There are some good small wall monuments, two heraldic paintings of merit and some prayer books dated 1778.

New Romney

Old Romney

Old Romney. St Clement. An irregular buttressed structure in fields neighboured by a large dark yew, which enhances the beauty of the warm yellows and browns of the lichen on the pale umber and silver stonework and shingled spire. The structure is largely of the thirteenth century. The interior is one of the best and least spoiled Georgian interiors in the country, giving an excellent idea of what a village church was like a hundred and fifty years ago. Most of the woodwork has been painted grey, which is effective. There is a Classic reredos, and there are simple Chinese-taste gates in the chancel arch. The Royal Arms hang over the chancel arch, and oval texts of the Marsh type are hung on each side of them and over the arcades. Clear glass in the windows, old floors, and indeed no visually disturbing feature at all. The church is well looked after. (Interior, plate 12.)

St Mary Marsh

RUCKINGE. St Mary Magdalene. Finely set, looking across the Marsh through the trees of the Royal Military Canal. The ballet-skirted spire with its lead pinnacle crowning it and the very wide roof covering the nave and south aisle give the exterior an attractive Kentish character. Two late Norman doorways add exterior richness, that on the south being of a fine colour with its lichen and texturing and pale-grey lead lintel. The interior is simple and whitewashed. The best internal features have, as at Warehorne, been removed and put away in the town – a fine eighteenth-century reredos with delicate painted marbling, and a magnificent florid Royal Arms. There are fragments of painted glass. The medieval features are not very rich.

ST MARY MARSH. A most textural exterior, the stonework washed and blown into a sculptural whole which nature has coloured most richly in warm grey-yellow and brown. There are thin but adequate thirteenth-

Snargate

and fourteenth-century, and later, features. The interior is simple and harmonious, with box pews (which may once have been painted white, as in W. D. Caröe's restoration at Fairfield), clear glass, white- and yellow-washed walls and arcade, and white-painted tower screen. It resembles a rural Norfolk church as drawn by Cotman. Brasses.

Snargate. St Dunstan. A picturesque church externally, breaking its back on the Marsh. The tower leans out, as at Newchurch. Thin, late features. There is a coarse but interesting painting of the Holy vessels in the north aisle. (Formerly there were two.) Nave and aisles, chancel, north tower, south porch. R. H. Barham was rector here, and Harold Gilman, painter, was son of a late rector.

Snave. St Augustine. Is picturesquely screened by trees in the marshy fields, and approached by a grass-grown avenue. It is very much Victorianized, and the interior so much so that all distinctive character has been removed. Nave, aisles, chancel, tower.

Snave

STONE-IN-OXNEY. St Mary. The church is a handsome fifteenth-century building, with western tower. It has been much Victorianized, and is notable chiefly for its exterior outline and texture.

WAREHORNE. St Matthew. There is much eighteenth-century work here, including the brick tower and north porch, incorporated into a fourteenth-century structure. There has been recent refurbishing. Twenty years ago the church had more character and was as worshipful. The eighteenth-century reredos and Commandment boards of a good simple type have been removed, though they still exist in the church and should be put back. The box pews luckily remain. There is fine fourteenth-century glass with figures in two north windows.

WEAT HYTHE. St Mary. A ruin, standing near the Military Canal, among a few houses and glasshouses. Roofless, and has been repaired at the west end. Some sparse remains of Norman work; but the building is chiefly of early fourteenth-century character.

Warehorne

FROM NEAR STONE

LYDD, ACROSS THE MARSH

THE MARSH NEAR APPLEDORE

LYDD-ON-SEA

LOOKING TOWARDS CAMBER

DUNGENESS

DUNGENESS FROM GALLOWAYS

FAIRFIELD

FAIRFIELD

IVYCHURCH

IVYCHURCH, NORTH AISLE

OLD ROMNEY

EAST GULDEFORD

THE ROYAL MILITARY CANAL NEAR LYMPNE

THE ROYAL MILITARY CANAL AT RUCKINGE

STUDFALL CASTLE AND LYMPNE